# WILD CANINES!

# FOXES

**By Jalma Barrett**
**Photographs by Larry Allan**

BLACKBIRCH PRESS, INC.
WOODBRIDGE, CONNECTICUT

Published by Blackbirch Press, Inc.
260 Amity Road
Woodbridge, CT 06525

**Email:** staff@blackbirch.com
**Web site:** www.blackbirch.com

Printed in the United States

10 9 8 7 6 5 4 3 2 1

**Dedication**
For Katlyn

–JB and LA

**Photo Credits**
All photographs ©Larry Allan, except for page 11 (inset): ©PhotoDisc.

**Library of Congress Cataloging-in-Publication Data**
Barrett, Jalma.
Foxes / text by Jalma Barrett : photographs by Larry Allan.
    p.   cm. — (Wild canines!)
   Includes bibliographical references.
   Summary: Describes the appearance, habits, hunting and mating tactics, family life, and life cycle of different species of foxes.
   ISBN 1-56711-263-3
   1. Foxes—Juvenile literature. [1. Foxes.] I. Allan, Larry, ill. II. Title. III. Series: Barrett, Jalma.  Wild canines!.
QL737.C22B343   2000
599.775—dc21
                          99-32641
                            CIP

# Contents

# Introduction

Walk into your backyard, or take a hike through the woods, and a pair of round fox eyes might be watching you from a nearby hiding place. These shy, unseen observers won't harm or threaten you. Foxes are found almost everywhere in North America, even in cities. There are four North American species—red fox, common gray fox, arctic fox, and kit or swift fox. Best known is the red fox. It inhabits the broadest North American territory of any of the foxes. It is also found in Europe and Asia.

Red foxes roam most of Canada and the United States, except in the West and Southwest. Gray foxes inhabit the eastern half of

**Where Foxes Are Most Common**

Canada

United States

Mexico

Central America

Fox territory

* Arctic fox

Red fox

▲ Kit fox

● Gray fox

the United States, as well as Oregon, California, Nevada, Utah, Colorado, Arizona, New Mexico, and Texas. They also live in Mexico and northern South America. Northern Canada and coastal Alaska's tundra (flat, treeless plains) and ice floes (frozen ocean water) are home to arctic foxes. They are also found in Greenland, Europe, and Asia. Recently classified by scientists as one species, kit and swift foxes live in Montana, Wyoming, Colorado, Idaho, Utah, Oregon, Nevada, and California. They are also found in the Canadian provinces of Alberta, Saskatchewan, and Manitoba.

Red foxes are one of four fox species found in North America.

# Physical Appearance

Foxes as a group share many physical traits. All are, on average, medium-sized mammals under 15 pounds (6.8 kilograms). They have long fur and bushy tails. Most foxes (except arctic foxes) have large, pointed ears, which provide them with excellent hearing.

Although they are physically similar to each other, each species of fox has a unique appearance. Red foxes have bushy tails measuring 14 to 17 inches (35–43 centimeters). They have rusty-brown heads and bodies, and are white on their chins, throats, and bellies. Red foxes are 15 to 16 inches (38–41 centimeters) tall. They weigh 8 to 15 pounds (3.5–7 kilograms). The backs of their ears, lower legs, and feet are black. Red foxes might also be black, silver, or a mixed pattern called a cross phase, which is reddish-brown with a dark fur cross on their shoulders.

All foxes share certain physical traits. Long fur and bushy tails are common to fox bodies.

Gray foxes have gray fur banded by reddish-brown, with black tips on their tails.

All color variations of red foxes have a white-tipped tail. They are the only species to have this kind of tail marking.

Gray foxes have gray fur on their backs, and reddish-brown on their sides, chests, necks, and backs of their heads. Their throats and bellies are white. Their bushy tails, 8 to 18 inches (22–44 centimeters) long, have a black stripe on the top and a black tip. Legs and feet are rusty red. They are 14 to 15 inches (36–38 centimeters) tall and weigh 7 to 13 pounds (3–6 kilograms).

Kit foxes are the smallest species of foxes.

Arctic foxes are bluish-brown or light gray with white on their undersides in summer. During winter, they change to all white or cream. This color change helps them blend well into their surroundings. They stand 10 to 12 inches (27–35 centimeters) tall and weigh 6 to 9 pounds (3–4 kilograms). Their bushy tails, ranging from 11 to 14 inches (27–35 centimeters), might have some black hairs on the tips. There is also a rare blue phase (dark bluish-gray), which lightens to pale blue-gray in winter. Arctic foxes' ears are small and rounded. Because there is less surface area for heat to escape, small ears help these foxes conserve body heat in winter.

Arctic foxes change color in summer and winter to blend with their surroundings.

Kit foxes are the smallest foxes. They have gray fur on their backs, yellow-tan fur on their sides, and whitish fur below. Their feet are light-colored and their ears are large and triangular. At 3 to 6 pounds (2–4 kilograms), kit foxes are about half the weight of the average house cat. They are about 12 inches (30 centimeters) tall with a 9- to 12-inch (23–30 centimeters) black-tipped tail.

# Special Features

All 4 species of foxes have excellent hearing. Unlike other mammals, a red fox's hearing is sensitive to low frequency sounds. They are able to hear small prey digging under the ground or snow, gnawing, or rustling.

Each fox species has special features that help it to survive in its particular environment. Most foxes will curl into a ball in winter, wrapping their tails over their noses and feet to protect themselves in cold and snowstorms. With a compact body, small ears, and short legs, an arctic fox is better able to retain body heat, making it especially well equipped for extreme cold. Their feet have thick fur, which protects them from cold and provides traction on ice. The kit fox is a particularly fast runner. It can reach 25 miles (40 kilometers) per hour for short distances. That is why it is also known as the "swift" fox. Gray foxes are the only species of canids that can climb trees.

Gray foxes are the only canids that can climb trees. They use their long back claws to dig into the bark as they climb.

With a compact body, small ears, and short legs, an arctic fox is designed to retain warmth in cold habitats.
**Inset:** An arctic fox curls itself into a tight ball to stay warm.

# Social Life

Most foxes prefer to be alone, except during mating season. Kit foxes and some gray foxes, however, will pair off for life. Males are called dogs. Females are called vixens. Baby foxes are called kits, which can be confusing because of the species called "kit" as well. Kit foxes got their name because, when full-grown, they are the size of kit foxes (young) from other species.

Fox territories are small. However, they carefully mark their boundaries with urine and feces (droppings). They spray urine on trees, bushes, or cacti; feces are often placed on rocks. This puts scents closer to nose level, and prevents the scent from being covered by snow or rain. The scent tells other foxes that the territory is taken.

**Opposite:** Territory is marked with urine and droppings, which have strong smells. These smells warn other foxes to stay away.

**Right:** Most foxes are solitary (prefer to be alone). Only during mating season do they pair off.

Because they are nocturnal (active mostly at night), foxes are not often seen by humans. Foxes also hide when they are frightened. During the day, foxes rest. One gray fox was spotted resting 30 feet (10 meters) up in a tree! Another was seen on the arm of a big, spiny, saguaro cactus!

Foxes "speak" with one another on many occasions. They communicate with various vocal cues, including whines, growls, yips, and barks. Yips indicate alarm. Foxes can't howl, but kits can purr. Gray foxes make cat-like yowls, but are not as vocal as red foxes.

# Hunting

Foxes are omnivores—animals that eat any sort of food. Their diets change with the seasons. In spring, foxes eat insects, grasses, berries, young rabbits and birds, eggs, and crayfish. In summer, they're almost vegetarians, eating corn, berries, apples, wild cherries, grapes, nuts, and grasses.

In late summer and early autumn, they also eat grasshoppers and crickets. In winter, foxes eat small mammals, including mice, rabbits, rats, ground squirrels, voles, woodchucks, lemmings, and carrion (already-dead meat). Arctic foxes also eat fish, and young seals and sea lions. Tiny kit foxes are mostly carnivores (meat eaters).

**Top:** When hunting larger prey, a fox will hide and wait for the right moment to jump out and charge.
**Left:** A red fox eats a squirrel. Most fox prey is small.
**Opposite:** A fox's diet is quite varied and will change with the seasons.

Foxes continue to hunt, even when they are well fed. Foxes cache (hide) food to get ready for winter. In summer, arctic foxes dig through the top layer of soil and place food on the permafrost (ground that remains frozen year-round). There the food is preserved as if it were in a freezer. Foxes also cache food in rock crevices and under rocks or snow. They return to their cache by memory and scent.

When hunting larger prey, like rabbits, red foxes are cat-like stalkers. They move in close to their intended victim, then run it down. Red foxes hunt in farmland, wooded areas, brush— even in cities and towns.

Gray foxes are not fast runners. They must surprise their prey.

Common gray foxes are slow runners. They must surprise their prey—that's why their well-camouflaged coats are a real help. They generally hunt in wooded or brushy areas, as well as in cities or towns.

The coloring of arctic foxes allows them to close in on prey without being seen. But they must ultimately chase it down. Although they are solitary, arctic foxes might gather around a large carcass to feed. They hunt on the tundra on the edge of northern forests, and will travel several hundred miles south to find food. During winter, they move far out on ice floes. Blue phase arctic foxes are not found where there is permanent snow cover. The darker coloring would be a disadvantage for hunting and hiding in a white world.

Kit foxes have extra fur between their toes to help prevent sinking in the sandy Southwestern areas where they hunt. Their diet includes lizards and scorpions, but their favorite food is the kangaroo rat. Kit foxes hunt in the short-grass prairies of the Great Plains, as well as in desert regions. They drink very little, getting the water they need from their food.

Foxes will often cache, or store, food during the summer or fall so they can survive the winter.
**Inset:** This arctic fox gets patches of blue fur in its coat as summer approaches.

# The Mating Game

Solitary foxes mate between January and April. Because of harsh weather, arctic foxes mate between February and May. Foxes reach sexual maturity at about 1 year. Gestation (length of time kits are carried in the mother's uterus) varies from 47 to 57 days. Foxes dig dens for raising their young shortly after they mate. They don't use nesting materials. Vixens keep the dogs out of the den before the young are born. Later, males bring food to their mates and newborns. Helper foxes (unbred females) also assist in caring for the kits. Dens have several openings. There are often alternative dens nearby to use in times of danger. Red foxes, who use the same dens for several years, often enlarge woodchuck or badger dens.

Most foxes are ready to begin mating at one year of age.

Arctic foxes dig new dens each year. In order to see in all directions, red foxes build dens on raised areas with sparse ground cover. Common gray foxes build dens in natural cavities in woodlands, on rock slopes, or in hollow logs and trees. Arctic foxes dig dens on sandy hillsides, or tunnel into snowbanks. Both parents care for the young. The male will guard the site. Kit foxes prefer to build dens in the open country. They are excellent diggers, and build dens that are usually 3 feet (1 meter) underground.

A young kit peers out from its den.

# Raising Fox Kits

One litter of 1 to 12 kits is produced each year, and they are born blind and helpless. Kit foxes have fewer young, usually 3 to 5. Kits are born from March through May. Arctic foxes give birth from April to July. Kits open their eyes at about 12 days, and are weaned at 3 months. Mothers chew and predigest the kits' first solid food. Then they regurgitate it (bring back from stomach to mouth) for their young. Parents bring food for 4 to 5 weeks, and it is given to the first kit who begs. Kits will usually step out of the den at 6 weeks of age. At first, parents may leave food near the entrance. Next, they'll hide a dead rabbit, squirrel, or bird a few feet from the entrance.

An 8-week-old red fox sits near the entrance of its den. At 6 weeks, a kit will make its first journey outside the den.

Gradually, they will move the food farther and farther away, encouraging the young to go out. Sometimes parents will bring live prey to the den so the kits can practice killing.

Parenting is a major chore—fox young eat about a pound of meat every 24 hours! Parents must catch between 500 and 600 rodents to feed their young for the 8 weeks the kits are in the den.

At about 4 months, kits begin to hunt with their parents at night. Young are taught how to find, stalk, and kill prey. Kits have strong hunting instincts—they pounce on insects and learn to pin them between their paws. Later, they learn how to kill field mice by biting their necks. The lessons stop at 7 months. That is when kits leave their families to establish their own territories. Young males might travel 150 miles (241 kilometers) from their parents' den; females remain closer. A few months later, they're ready to begin the cycle of life all over again, this time as parents.

Play wrestling and chasing help a kit develop the strength and skills it will need to hunt in the wild.

# Foxes and Humans

A fox has many natural enemies, including wolves, coyotes, bobcats, and lynx. But a fox's primary enemy is humans. Lack of knowledge and understanding of foxes causes people to shoot and trap them. Trapping and bounty hunting (killing animals for payment) has claimed hundreds of thousands of foxes over the years. But people today are not buying fur, or fur-trimmed, coats as frequently as in the past. Fox populations are growing, except for the threatened kit fox. Poultry farmers, too, are no longer as quick to destroy foxes.

Humans are the single most dangerous predators for foxes.

Today, farms are more predator-proof, so there is less need to kill foxes to protect farm animals. Red foxes are currently expanding their territory and competing with coyotes for former wolf territory. Arctic foxes are still being trapped for their unusually long fur, especially in the blue phase. Arctic foxes are raised commercially because their pelts (skin on fur-bearing animals) are valuable.

Cunning, shy, and seldom-seen, foxes are valuable contributors to life in North America. As skilled predators in the food chain, they help maintain the proper balance of nature. And, even though their pelts may bring high prices, foxes are far more valuable for the unique role they play in the natural world.

## Fox Facts

**Scientific Name:** Red—*Vulpes vulpes*
Arctic—*Alopex lagopus*
Common Gray—*Urocyan cinereoargenteus*
Kit—*Vulpes velox*

**Shoulder Height:** 10" to 16" (26–41 centimeters)

**Body Length:** 24" to 44" (61–113 centimeters)

**Tail Length:** 9" to 18" (23–44 centimeters)

**Weight:** 3 to 15 pounds (2–7 kilograms)

**Color:** Shades of gray, red, white, tan, black, and silver

**Gestation:** 47 to 57 days

**Litters Born:** 1 per year

**Litter Size:** 1 to 12 kits

**Social Life:** Solitary, except during mating season

**Favorite Food:** Varied diet—vegetarian, small mammals, insects, birds, eggs, and crayfish

**Range:** Generally throughout North America, including Arctic regions

# Glossary

**ambush** To hide and then attack.

**cache** To hide; a hidden supply.

**feces** Bodily wastes; droppings.

**frequency** Repeated vibrations.

**ice floe** Frozen ocean water.

**inhabit** To live in a certain area or location.

**nocturnal** Active at night.

**solitary** Living and hunting alone.

**stalking** To hunt or track in a quiet, secret way; usually following prey.

**tundra** A cold, treeless area where the soil under the ground surface is permanently frozen.

**weaned** No longer breastfeeding.

# For More Information

## Books

Butterworth, Christine. Donna Bailey (Contributor). *Foxes* (Animal World). Chatham, NJ: Steck-Vaughn Library Division, 1991.

Lepthien, Emilie. Joan Kalbacken. *Foxes* (New True Book). Danbury, CT: Children's Press, 1993.

Tweit, Susan. Wendy Shattil (Photographer). *City Foxes*. Seattle, WA: Alaska Northwest Books, 1997.

## Web Site

*Family Canidae*

Find out more about the fox family and its relatives— sciweb.onysd.wednet.edu/sciweb/zoology/mammalia/dog.html.

# Index